Don't Blame Me

A seriously cynical, accurate, and sometimes
funny book about how NOT to live life

Rosalie Brown

ISBN: 0692963561

ISBN-13: 978-0692963562

Dedication

For the girls I love most on this planet, Hayden & Zara.

ROSALIE BROWN

Acknowledgements

To the people in my life who tolerate all my nonsense, but most definitely Renee, Valerie, Shanin and Lydia.

And for my psychic friends network...

CONTENTS

INTRODUCTION

What's the Big Idea?

Listen, I'm not qualified to write a self-help book. So, it's a good thing that this is NOT a self-help book.

I have never had a life plan, and even if I had a plan, I would never remember it. I am most certainly not a therapist, counselor, priest, or even a very compassionate or likable person (no matter what I post on Facebook).

I have screwed up, squeaked by, and literally done thousands of stupid things that strangers on the internet have found quite alarming, and sometimes entertaining. Now, just think of all the stupidity you can avoid for yourself just by leafing through this book!

Here's how I do/don't do life. **You're welcome.** *Don't Blame Me.*

ROSALIE BROWN

Chapter One

DON'T SLEEP YOUR WAY TO THE TOP: LIE TO THE MIDDLE

Lie. That's right. Don't lie to other people, just lie to yourself. Now, there are some drawbacks to this approach, but I won't kid you...it has always sort of worked out for me. This approach will make the staunchly honest, and highly educated person, well, nervous. But if you tell yourself something long enough, guess what happens? You start to believe it.

Listen, I started college. I was actually OK at college. And I always imagined I'd be the college grad in the family. It wasn't a big competition. My brother made that easy on me. He was really good at selling weed. Back when weed was illegal across all 50 states.

As of this writing, I can't keep track of where weed is legal and where it gets you jail time. I guess that's good for everyone – job security for the police and corrections officers. By the way, I have zero to say on those career choices, other than...better you than me. I am more of a sucker punch and run and hide sort of person, than a law and order, justice at all costs sort of person.

Now, criminality does sort of run in my family. What I learned from my brother's criminal endeavors was basically this: Don't Get Caught. Seems easy, but bro just couldn't seem to succeed there. Not an overachiever, more of a repeat offender.

Back in the day, we had a thing called "Three Strikes" and if you got in trouble, you guessed it, three times, you were basically at the mercy of the sentencing laws in your state. If you got arrested for drugs, sometimes you got drug rehab, but my brother was sort of a quitter. He kept quitting rehab. Needless to say, I learned a lot about what not to do in life. Thanks, bro! (It's OK for me to share all this. We no longer speak, and he is still a dick).

Surrounded by such rich life experiences, I decided early on I would not be a criminal. I was going to be an overachiever and go to college.

So, I got the grades and did the whole college tour thing...but guess what sometimes happens when you have a brother who is a criminal? Sometimes they steal money from your parents, to the tune of several hundreds of thousands of dollars, and...suddenly, there's no money for college for the smart kid in the family.

In this case, I was the smart kid. I had done A/P courses, had extra credits for college, and yet, couldn't pay for college because mom and pop were facing bankruptcy. Don't tell me weed doesn't ruin lives I'm still slightly irritated, perhaps even bitter, about this whole episode.

So off to community college I went. I was a bit of an underachiever in community college, because I left home a bit pre-maturely and freedom tasted more fun than going to classes. I worked about 3 jobs at a time, telling myself I'd keep up with my studies...but guess who discovered the wonders of marijuana?

Oh, yes...I suddenly got it. And I realized maybe I should have been nicer to my weed selling brother.

After a short stint at college, I realized you could actually make a little money selling weed. My brother wasn't a complete idiot. Though I was not a very good "criminal," I did OK with the three jobs, the money from the weed, and partying whenever I got the chance. Or so I thought.

One day I woke up and realized, *holy crap*, I had accidentally dropped out of college. At least that's what the letter from the college said. I don't remember making a decision to drop out, but basically, me and college "broke up." One of several break-ups, something that would become a recurring theme throughout my life. Yeah! I was going to be good at something, finally.

Entering the job market was not new to me, but I didn't have a career. It was basically a series of retail-ish and restaurant-ish jobs that when cobbled together, allowed me to sleep on the couches of friends, and smoke a lot of weed. But I'd have to be an adult sooner or later, damn it.

I pulled out the classified section of the newspaper. For anyone under the age of 30 who might be browsing this book while in line at the bookstore, allow me to explain what the classified section was. Back in the day, we read these things, printed on paper, called "newspapers." And inside said "newspapers" were these things called news stories, written by "journalists" and in the back, they featured advertisements for things like jobs and apartments and cars.

Perusing the advertisements for jobs, I realized that perhaps completing college might have given me more of an advantage. I couldn't really put "weed dealer" on my resume, and saying I was a cashier at a restaurant, or a parking attendant at the concert venue probably wouldn't open many doors. Probably.

But what if I was so much more? What if, for example, I was a supervisor at a busy restaurant? Or what if I was a manager at the concert venue? I wouldn't come out and say I was a college graduate, mainly because I wasn't even old enough to be graduated yet. But I always excelled at creative writing, and that my friend, is where I focused my energies. Being creative. With truth and facts and experiences. I became the most interesting person I knew. Even if I was 85% made up!

Had I led fundraising campaigns to help orphans? You bet. Did I know how to manage a multi-million dollar operating budget? Of course. Was I experienced in dealing with very difficult clients? Duh.

And guess who fast tracked their ass right into management positions? This fraud. Now back then, we didn't have this glorious internet thing, and fact checking was really just a Human Resources rep making a phone call to some person whose name and number YOU supplied, and that person the HR rep called could be anyone. Literally, anyone! (Thanks Tiffany!)

So, I started getting jobs that I was woefully unqualified for. And when I say woefully, that might be an understatement. I was at one point a Fundraising Manager, Fundraising Director, Marketing Director, Advertising Director, Agency Owner, and so many more things.

Did I make it rich? Well, nope. My climb to the top was a bit scary at times, mostly me being scared of being discovered as a total fraud. But it also made me hustle. And, obviously got me to stop selling weed. *Kids, don't sell weed*. Even if it does happen to be legal where you are, which of course seems to change from election cycle to election cycle. Don't bank on making it rich off pot. Plus, not to sound like a jaded adult, but there are things like taxes and stuff that the government expects you to pay, and life just gets easier if you live a pretty boring and reliable life.

Each job, though perhaps initially earned illegitimately, did give me a better jumping off point. I could climb the corporate (and non-profit) ladder by building off each job/lie.

In my defense, I did pick up amazing on-the-job training that gave me tons of experience, and by the end of my corporate tenure, I wasn't really a liar anymore. I did have years of experience doing corporate stuff, and I was pretty good at a whole lot of it.

You probably shouldn't lie...I mean, maybe it's OK when you're going to earn a living. People really just want "yes" people anyway. So "yes" your ass into that dream job, get some experience, and make some dollars. It's a win-win for everyone. To all the careers that I fibbed my way into...thanks for giving me a chance. And you're welcome, because I was always awesome.

Lying doesn't always turn out badly. Except when it does. To the lawyer type folks out there, I don't need any more hate mail, and no, I am not advocating crime or fraud. I am however advocating lying to yourself when it serves you, and being as creative as possible, whenever possible. If you don't believe in yourself, who will?

Chapter Two

DON'T BELIEVE IN "HAPPILY EVER AFTER"

Let's be real. There is no such thing as a fairytale, unless you of course work at the movie studios and that's your job, making fairytales come to life. In the "real world" as I like to call my shit show of a life, fairytales are things you read to small children. (Reading is important, kids).

Maybe you were raised around loving, supportive family members who modeled healthy marriages. If so, you should skip over this section, because none of this will make sense to you.

I did grow up around a lot of married people, including the jokers that I called parents. They were my adoptive parents who eventually decided they weren't my "real" parents, as if you get an escape clause with parenting...but whatever. Years of therapy have helped me greatly with this – and they are no longer referred to as the "assholes," simply the "jokers." Yes, therapy pays off sometimes. If nothing else, it's comforting to be able to have a complete nervous breakdown, week after week, with no judgment, at just $175 a visit. Bargain!

But I digress. My parents were married but hated each other, and actually they hated pretty much everyone. During my childhood I decided getting married was what you did when you really hated someone. *I had cracked the code to adulthood!* Find someone you hate, and marry them. And if you wanted to be an overachiever, make sure you added kids to the equation. The American Dream!

At the tender age of 19, I met a horrible human being and decided, *"Wow, I totally hate you! Of course, I'll marry you."* And there you have it, American Dream achieved. But not until I left 27 times and went back, which led to make up sex, which led to creating a human! I had achieved more by 20 years old than most little girls could only imagine while they were being read fairytales.

Find a total jackass whom you hate. Check. Be sure to have emotional, mental and financial instability. Check. Make a baby with this ridiculous person. Check. Drown all your troubles with weed. Damn it, I was a parent. Uncheck.

You can imagine that with such a tainted view of "adulting," which was not a legitimate term back then, my efforts at adulthood were not epic successes. Lest you forget, I'm an overachiever. I never did anything small. And I made sure that no matter what kind of help people offered me, I had to turn it away. I was going to be the best god damn unhappy adult that ever decided to adult!

So, what are you to take from my story? *Ah, this is why this author is so bitter and messed up.* No, that's not the moral of the story. The moral of the story is...DON'T BELIEVE WHAT YOU WERE TAUGHT TO BELIEVE. That applies to damn near every situation.

Happily ever after is a bunch of bullshit, because life is dangerous and wild and magnificent and crazy. But marriage does not have to be a hate-hate situation, like I was raised to believe. And having kids and getting divorced does not mean the end of the world.

It's also not necessarily how every marriage goes, or ends, as it were. Though, let's discuss the astounding divorce rates in this country (over 60%!). I mean, I get it, people suck and being around the same person all the time is sure to drive anyone nuts, but are we just throwing in the towel and giving up because the person we married has bad habits or is an asshole before coffee? Or are people just not wired to be monogamous? That's probably a discussion for much brighter minds than mine.

I'll stick to what I know: life can get hard, but you're harder.

I know how that sounds. But think about it. You've made it through every one of your hardest days so far, right? So just keep going. Marriages don't always mean parenthood; marriages don't always mean divorce; and your wedding picture really doesn't need to be over your mantle after the first year, in my opinion.

Life is full of risks. You can take the easy road like I did. I knew what to expect when I married someone I hated. I was going to have a marriage much like my parents. That was a conscious choice. I own it, I celebrate it, and actually my kid is fucking awesome, so I don't regret any of it. What's all this mean to you?

I think if you and I met, we might be friends. If you have an annoying voice or call me too much, it probably wouldn't work out…but let's pretend we are friends. What I would say to you is this: love yourself, possibly another human if they come along, and if it doesn't work out like you hoped, short periods of binge drinking and therapy can be super helpful. That was how I spent the majority of my twenties, part of my thirties, and it's certainly working OK in my forties.

Fuck the Fairytale! (Remember, this isn't a self-help book).

Chapter Three

DON'T DATE IF YOU'RE A DIVORCEE (WITH A KID)

Don't.

Seriously. This could be the shortest chapter ever written on a topic that at least 60 percent (probably more!) of the US population will be faced with. I can tell you it is one of the dumbest, worst things you can do.

Dating sucks in general. Now with the beauty of the internet and picture apps (filters!), and the creative writers that abound on every corner of the globe...you too can date a totally fictitious person! Who knows, maybe you'll even get a celebrity to fall in love with you.

But we already covered fairytales. (See previous chapter). Dating has become a billion-dollar industry (I have no idea, but I think I read that somewhere reputable.) Everyone is looking for love.

They don't look in the mirror for love, they run to dating apps looking for validation and "likes" on social media selfies, the ones with the perfect lighting and amazing angles.

Your best dating years, I hate to break it to you, are in your twenties. You aren't wrinkled or saggy or flabby yet; your skin still bounces back; you're not totally bitter and broken at twenty-five, you have years ahead of you to get broken and bitter. Now that's a fun ride! Buckle up, Buttercup!

In your twenties you still think anything is possible, that you're immortal, that you won't be crushed by debt, despair, depression. The young really do have it all, don't they? But here's another interesting fact about people in their twenties: they sort of, kind of don't like themselves, because they think they're supposed to be something more.

 When you hit your forties, you just sort of accept that life is a rollercoaster and Plan A sometimes becomes Plan C or Plan D, and if you survive, you might be doing something right.

When you are dating in your thirties and forties, you're faced with prospective mates that have probably been married and divorced already, possibly have children, and sometimes with children comes the proverbial insane ex. So, it's a different game.

Not only do you have to get your prospective mate to like you,

you probably need to win over a child or teenager (good luck!), and you're walking into a situation that includes an ex-wife or ex-husband, and sometimes they are the spawn of Satan. So, there is a lot to look forward to! Good luck, Cupcake!

So why do we bother? Because it is in our DNA to be coupling up on some level. Most of us like sex, or used to, and some of us aren't ashamed to admit it, while others seek out company of the opposite sex/same sex, because they truly want to share their lives with another human. I personally believe that a brick to the head, and adopting a dog, are much better options. Less pain, more loyalty.

You may meet some amazing people when you're dating. And you are most definitely going to meet some weirdos. If you're like me, you take note and you make sure you include some of those stories in your memoirs or (non) self-help books.

One of my favorite weird dates happened in the not so very distant past. I met Paul through an online dating app, and at this point in my life, I wasn't putting looks first, although he was a solid 6.4 and he probably felt similarly. (I'm not going to stop traffic, and I'm not getting any younger, though I am a total bad ass). We met for dinner after several brief emails. I had learned through experience it's not a bad idea to keep everything through email and not give out your phone number before the date, thereby avoiding the constant texters.

Let me be very clear, and possibly serve as a warning to you single/uncoupled people: like many grown adults: I don't care for clingy, text you every second of the day, pretend we know each other even though we've never met, kind of interactions. And especially not when it makes me want to throw my smart phone under a bus.

If you've ever participated in online dating, you may be aware, the ocean of online daters are all about the texting thing. It's annoying, and you should stop.

Did I mention that I hate when people try to get to know you through texting? This bullshit creates false intimacy and leads people to think they know each other. Incorrect. You know their phone number and perhaps that they can offer clever one liners on a semi-consistent basis. This does not a relationship make. But I digress.

Back to Paul, the most boring dater in my history of dating. We met for dinner and he spoke incessantly about the recent election (I had baited breathe, afraid to find out if he voted for the derelict who had just stolen the election). He wanted to be the smarty in the room, and with me, that takes a lot. Because I am not only a smart ass, I am actually fairly smart, despite the number of times I use vernacular incorrectly, or speak like a child of the 80s.

He rambled on and on and was boring me to tears, but dinner was pretty good, and I was hungry. He was definitely paying, not because I am a gold digger (it was a $12 dinner), but because that was part of his thing – "look at me, I can treat a lady!" Meh. I kept wondering why the conversation was so one sided, and then I'd sort of given up giving two fucks, because after all, dinner was pretty good, and I was super hungry.

Finally, after 45 minutes, he said, "So I understand that you are a web developer and you work at Blah Blah Blah and you live in Blah Blah Blah...what's that like?"

Tip: This is **<u>NOT</u>** how you impress a lady, or me. Up until dinner Mr. Web Detective only knew my first name, didn't have my phone number, and I definitely had not shared where I lived or what I did for a living.

Before I could say anything, he volunteered that using my first name and email address he'd done an internet search to find out who I was. Now that's sexy. Except, it's really not. So*, you didn't ask me any questions about myself during dinner because you did a Google search, and you think you know everything about me?* Damn it, let's get married.

In a perfect world, I would say, that was our last date. But I am an imperfect person, and I like to eat. So, we had two more, almost as painful dates, before I actually had to explain to him we had zero chemistry and there was no sense wasting each other's time. Which considering, I thought was pretty mature of me. Because what I wanted to say was: "You suck at dating!" But to be fair, I pretty much suck at dating, too.

I think most people suck at dating. So, what are your options? Well I did meet a husband at a bar. Not someone else's husband, to be clear...the guy that would become lucky husband #2. Yes, I've been married twice. And if you're following along, you may have deduced, divorced twice. There really are worse things, I promise you.

The people you meet at bars are generally pretty clear, they want to get laid. Perhaps you'll hear from them again, perhaps you won't, but the one thing they want is to get naked. And I'm not judging. I did have a life back in my twenties, and I actually married one of those bar people. Of course, we both did a lot of drinking back then, he still drinks, but that's another story.

There is nothing wrong with getting laid, in fact, I highly recommend it. But people often have conflicting interests. People can present themselves as "looking for a relationship" when what they really mean is "looking for a lay." We really shouldn't make people feel like they have to hide their motives, but no one wants to be judged for wanting temporary companionship versus a possible commitment. Naturally, they flock to dating apps where everyone is trying to be the "perfect one."

I can't say I have never had positive dating experiences, they have just been much more elusive than the regrettable ones. I am not sure that's unique, on the contrary, statistically speaking, dating is shitty and every once in a while, you get a quick glimmer of hope. That hope can all go up in smoke when you ignore your list of deal breakers.

Everyone has deal breakers. Once you start to ignore those, you're screwed. If you ever log onto a dating website, you'll notice a pattern: everyone has a list of must haves and must nots. It's only humorous until you recognized how fucked up a world we must live in that people have to spell out things like:

- No prison time
- No prison tatts
- No face tatts
- No kids (if you're over the age of 30, good luck with that!)
- No crazy exes (again, if you're over 30, fat chance!)
- No weird fetishes
- No cats

Sometimes you have to go through some crazy shit, to figure out what your deal breakers are. I genuinely never thought I'd have to specify "no prison time," but that really is a thing that is best spelled out. I never imagined I'd have to say no communicable diseases, but then again, I am a dreamer, if nothing else.

While creative photos and creative storytelling have become the reality of online dating, it's not always much better in real world dating situations. I especially love the part of the date, after the dinner and drinks, when the bill arrives, and the guy says, *"So we're splitting this right?"*

Or maybe even better is when your date says, *"Let's meet up at 1pm,"* and you arrive to find your charming suitor actually got there at 10am, and has been slamming vodka tonics for the past 3 hours. Arriving to find a slurring, sloppy mess at 1pm on a Sunday is absolute bliss! Mama never told me I'd have dates like this! Woohoo!

Let's cut to the chase...you know who the perfect one for you is? I don't either, but if you look in the mirror you will probably find them. Dating is a process of activities, companionship, and hopefully sex. But not every person you date is someone you want to have your home address.

You may wonder, what's my point? That I suck at dating? Oh, I have a ton of dating stories, way worse than "Paul." In fact, many of my experiences now just have labels in my memory box, labeled by the person's most annoying quality.

For example, here are just a few:

- Guy with severe lisp (also known as Lispy)

- Lives in Van at River (homeless but had a smart phone)

- Angry Military Guy (wanted to be called Sarge)

- Guy Who Was Married and Failed to Mention It

- Mr. Huge Teeth (simply could not look past his mouth)

Busted, I really suck at dating. I have collected a shit ton of awful experiences, that I will probably hold onto forever and discuss at length with future therapists. However, I did learn some stuff.

I should mention, even though I have painted myself as a shallow, gold digging (hot food!), bad dater, I have had some enjoyable dating. But I don't think it ever started online. My friends and I have heard of people meeting and falling in love from dating apps, but when put on the spot, we have a difficult time remembering who those happy couples are. But, of course it must happen to some. Just not most.

I whole heartedly believe that if you want to date so you can avoid being alone or lonely, **stop yourself**. That's the worst reason to go looking for love. If you have a void inside (and lots of us do), allow a word of caution: you'll never fill your void with someone else. You'll start accepting behaviors or things you'd never be OK with, simply to avoid losing the attention you're getting for someone else. You'll start bargaining behaviors and actions, and you'll settle. Bargain basement settle, if you're not careful.

If you want to date because you enjoy people, enjoy being alone, and have a healthy balance of alone time and party time, then you might be doing it right. And look, I told you at the beginning of the book, I have zero professional training, but I do know some shit.

I don't really believe anyone wants to be alone, and most the time, that's driven by fear. Fear of missing out, fear of dying alone, fear of Christmas with the family...it takes many forms. (Flasks can be extremely helpful in navigating family gatherings, in case you weren't aware).

To date successfully, I suggest being totally cool with who you are, being able to have fun whether you're alone or with friends, and it seems like a good time to mention the flask again. Flasks aren't just for the holidays. If dating teaches us anything it's that people are crazy, and dating people means going on a drunken adventure of epic proportions. On the upside, you just might get laid.

Chapter Four

DON'T LEAVE YOUR UNDERWEAR BEHIND

Seriously. It's a bad move. No matter what you've seen in movies, it's really not cute, or charming, or non-psychotic. There are two ways you can handle this: 1) don't wear underwear at all or 2) take them with you when you go.

After a chapter telling you that there is no such thing as "happily ever after," and a chapter on why you shouldn't date, you might assume I am anti-sex. That is not the case. Like most adult humans on the planet, I'm a fan of sex. It's fun, it feels good, and if you are doing it right, you probably sleep better.

So, I'd never advise you to give up on sex, but if it involves another person, there will come a moment when the drawers get dropped and for a lot of people, underwear will come off too. I don't believe in leaving anyone behind, especially underwear, or my phone number. But for now, we'll just talk underwear.

A lot of women, so I've been told, like to feel sexy and do so simply by wearing expensive underwear. When I was young, I too spent $18 for a pair of lace that barely covered my lady bits, in anticipation of that *"oh wow, look at your snatch!"* encounter that might happen at any given moment.

I am not saying I was a slut when I was young, and I know that no one thinks "slut shaming" is a good idea, but the 80s and 90s were a different time, and I ended up showing off my expensive underwear way less than I thought I would, and simultaneously, way more than perhaps I should have. But again, that was a different time. And I sure as hell wasn't going to leave $18 underwear behind.

When I adulted and became a parent, my focus shifted from lace underwear (let's be honest, the underwear already did its job – I did get knocked up, after all!) to looking for value packs of underwear, 6 stuffed in plastic packaging for $12 a pop.

I no longer got my underwear at Victoria's Secret, or even at the Mall. It was Target and Walmart and places that bundled cheap cotton underwear in packs.

What could be worse than leaving your expensive, lacy lingerie behind? Leaving stretched, cotton "mom" underwear behind. That would be worse. In my infinite wisdom, I just stopped wearing underwear all together. Not only was it cheaper, and every once in a while, more efficient, but it was pretty liberating to be commando while my friends were all fretting about panty lines and the inevitable itch that came with those horrible G-strings.

No lines for me! No itch! No more cotton mom briefs.

However, for those who still insist on wearing underwear, I do know what I'm talking about when I urge you not to leave your underwear behind as a kind of sad, desperate "calling card."

Once, when I was a young, adventurous person in the 90s, I ended up going home with some guy after a night of drinking far too much brown liquor. I think a friend of mine came along too, but only because we drove together. Anyway, when I woke up in the closet, with a Dirt Devil sticking in my back, I realized that I not only had no idea where I was, I had no idea where my underwear were. Gasp.

One could argue that my underwear was the least of my issues that cold, dark, hungover morning. And they would be right, I was definitely focused on the wrong issue. At the time, I was troubled that my underwear were missing, probably hiding next to my dignity.

Realizing that the priority was to exit the closet (*where in the hell was I?*), find my friend and her car keys, and get the hell out of there, I groped around in the dark and grabbed the first pair of underwear my hand landed on. Thankfully, shame produces its own brand of quiet, and the car ride home was forgettable and no words were exchanged. When I reached my apartment door, I looked down to find the underwear clutched in my hand. They weren't mine.

That could have been the very last time I ever wore underwear, I can't say for sure. But it was most definitely the last time I ever woke up in a closet. It was also the last time I ever drank brown liquor of any kind, which was probably not a coincidence.

I don't know if that guy ever found my underwear, or if the woman (presumably) who had worn the underwear clutched in my hungover hand, ever wondered what became of her lacey unmentionables, but it was the underwear fiasco that changed my life and ultimately led me to "team commando."

Now imagine being the guy who wakes the next morning and finds his overnight companion has gone home, but her underwear stayed behind. In fact, I don't have to imagine, because one of my dearest male friends was that guy. And the woman who left the underwear behind was a psycho. They do make for the best stories, fortunately.

When they went to bed, their relationship was undefined, but once the underwear got left behind, everything changed. She began calling and texting and messaging on social media. She wanted those underwear back. What she really wanted was to see him again, but instead of just saying, *"hey, I had a great time, can we get together again?"* her messages were all about getting her underwear back. Which made her start to seem really weird. They were just underwear. Don't be that girl.

She started off trying to be cute, which rarely works. After about the 10th message about underwear, my friend had no choice but to decide if it would be easier to just mail her these magic underwear, send her a gift certificate to the Mall to replace the magic underwear, or just block her on social media and every device he had. Guess what he chose? (After all of our friends screamed "THIS ISN'T ABOUT UNDERWEAR.")

If you take anything from this chapter, please let it be: it's just underwear. Don't lose your dignity, your friends, or potential sexual partners, over underwear.

Chapter Five

DON'T TAKE YOUR EYES OFF YOUR DRINK

(OR YOUR HANDS OFF MY ASS)

When you're going through a divorce, the best thing you can do for yourself is to go chase some tail. Be careful with what you catch. Seriously, it's good for you to remember that you're a warm-blooded human who is not destined to die alone. Even if you end up sleeping with some idiots, the important thing is to keep your head in the game. But don't take your eyes off your drink, because if you do, there are likely to be lots of idiots, and sometimes really excruciating hangovers.

When I was young, it was really easy to get a guy to buy me drinks, especially when I was underage. While that may speak to the disgusting predatory nature of some people, it got me through my late teens, and I have come to appreciate those days for what they were – horrible, shameful mistakes. Again, therapy has helped. (Therapy does get expensive!)

When my husband and I split, I found myself with lots of freedom and time on my hands. It was not a bad time, to be honest. Except for that one time. As far as I knew, I'd never taken drugs without my consent, and I'd only heard about GHB on crime documentaries and the evening news. Being far past the legal drinking age, I no longer got excited when someone offered me free liquor, because I was capable of buying my own. That's not 100% true, I did like it when I didn't have to spend $8 on cheap cranberry juice and cheaper vodka.

I was new to blind dates and still not completely jaded. So, when a co-worker that I knew marginally set me up on a blind date with that really "worldly" guy who spent his days designing TV sets and nights designing clothes, the first thought in my mind was not, "*Wait, is he straight?*" My first thought was, "*Fashion! Something I know nothing about, how cool!*"

I can say unequivocally that he was in fact straight. Ok, well not unequivocally, because we didn't actually make it to first base after I threw up on the side of his car for about 12 miles…but I'm still sure he was straight. Jumping ahead!

We had agreed to meet up downtown after I finished Christmas shopping for my kids. They were spending a few days with their dad and I was all about spoiling the hell out of them, our first Christmas as a "broken" family. The kids were pretty excited about getting twice the gifts. We all cope in our own special way.

When I met up with the blind date at the bar it was still early and we both felt free to go running and screaming back to our own cars if necessary. I remember thinking he looked a bit like Dave Matthews with a 5 o'clock shadow.

When I was exploring my "single" self, I discovered that I had a thing for musicians. Really one in particular. Eddie Vedder from Pearl Jam. *(They were inducted into the Rock n' Roll Hall of Fame in 2017, so yes, they are still together, making music, and relevant).*

Truthfully my go-to would be Mr. Vedder, even though arguably he is shorter than me, more morose than I, and married to a super model. It might come as no surprise then that Mr. Vedder has come up in my dating life more than once.

One time when I was breaking things off with an abnormally weird guy, he became very emotional and blurted out, *"You're breaking up with me because I don't look like Eddie Vedder!"* Wow. No, loose cannon, I broke up with you because you'd say stupid things like that. No one looks like Eddie Vedder, besides Eddie Vedder.

Another time Mr. Vedder came up was during an awkward first

and last date. The guy had noticed a Pearl Jam decal on my car and so he led with "My roommate is friends with Eddie Vedder's uncle. His name is Freddie." Of course, Eddie had an uncle named *Freddie*. That doesn't sound made up at all, and of course that sort of thing would impress me. (You can't see my eye roll, but trust me, it was epic).

Jesus, forget dating, just give me batteries. That was the last time I ever saw the guy, although I often wonder about the opportunities I passed up, what with his roommate being friends with Eddie Vedder's uncle, and what not. But I digress, again.

Pleasantly surprised to be face to face with a less musical, but sort of resembling, Dave Matthews, the first date was off to a good start. We had easy conversation, he commented that I looked like I had a runner's body *(what a load of crap!)* and he noticed I had no panty lines *(see, commando!)*. At that time in my life, that was a good date.

We had a couple of cheap drinks, although he was paying, and moved to a more upscale bar that had recently opened. Suddenly we were surrounded by a new crowd, upscale, chatty and well dressed. I was just buzzed enough to find everyone enjoyable, which should have alerted me I was probably more than buzzed. Since I typically find most people annoying.

My date had his hand on the small of my back, which sometimes went down to my ass (again, no panty lines!), and I was feeling good. And then the guy next to us started buying us drinks. A more savvy dater might have recognized it was a bit unusual for a single guy to become infatuated with the couple sitting next to him, but I was anything but savvy. Maybe it wasn't so unusual, and I just wasn't worldly enough to recognize what was coming.

I had always been super dense when it came to possible threesomes. I was 17 years old and that short guy in Hall & Oates wanted to bang me and my friend in his hotel room. At the same time. I sort of get it now, being old. I was young and tall and red headed, which some people found attractive. Like short, middle-aged, washed up, rock stars.

 How did I get propositioned by a washed-up rock star? I was working back stage at a concert venue with a friend of mine, who was also a red head, about 20 years old, and close to six feet tall. When he asked us to go back to his hotel room, Suzie got the drift, whereas I was totally clueless. Not interested, but clueless.

Once Suzie explained, using hand gestures, what he was asking for, I was grossed out. He was short! And over forty! Did people really do that?

Years later, I remained clueless, but I understood the logistics without hand gestures. After this stranger kept buying me and my date drinks, we finally figured out that there was something going on, so we got out of there and walked to a local 24-hour diner, leaving the prospect of the threesome behind.

What I didn't know was that the stranger was putting GHB in my drinks. This would turn out badly for everyone. Except the stranger who was totally unscathed.

While sitting at the diner waiting on menus, I suddenly couldn't see anything. My eyes were open and I could hear what my date was saying, but I had no ability to speak (or see), and warn him that I was definitely about to throw up all over the table. I can only imagine the look of terror on the man's face as I chucked up all over the table.

I felt his hand on the small of my back (no panty line!) as he rushed me out to his car, and I heard him ask me desperately, *"Do you think you could remember how to get home? AND CAN YOU ROLL DOWN YOUR WINDOW?!"*

This kind soul, who sadly remained a stranger after our one, epic evening together, was able to navigate all the way to my house, while I made grunting sounds between pukes. I can sort of recall his hand steadying mine as I put the key into my front door and mumbled something about my car being left downtown. He pushed me inside, slammed the door and sped away, as any normal human would have.

Apparently, I puked my way to my bedroom, crawled inside my bed, and woke up 2 days later, not sure what had happened. If not for the pukes in the living room, hallway, and bedroom, I would have erased the entire incident from my memory.

As one might assume, they were the worst couple days of my life, with the most epic hangover, and disgusting housekeeping duties ever. Death would have been a welcome turn of events.

The moral of the story is DON'T TAKE YOUR EYES OFF YOUR DRINK. And, again, you feel sexier when you don't wear any underwear at all, even when you wake up in puke.

Chapter Six

DON'T SKIMP ON THE REALLY IMPORTANT STUFF

Nope. I'm not talking about sentimental stuff. I am talking about the really important stuff. Like the things that bring you joy. Or things that give you life. Or things that keep your privates from getting chaffed. Never should you ever buy cheap toilet paper. I cannot relate to anyone who buys single ply toilet paper, and unfortunately you usually don't discover your friend is a single ply(er) until you're squatting on their pot, and you have no choice but to annihilate your vagina or your ass. These people should not be in your life.

Women go through a lot to keep themselves pretty from the waist down, well some women. There is shaving and waxing and trimming...the amount of time that women put into keeping their vaginas attractive is in total contrast to the amount of time actually spent looking at the vagina. I can't speak for everyone of course, but I've never found that the time balanced out.

But I ask you, after all that time and effort spent on vaginal grooming, why in the world would you settle for sandpaper on your toilet paper roll? The $2 you save at the super market has absolutely zero equivalency in the real world. Doesn't it just make sense? Spend the extra two dollars!

Another area where you should never skimp is coffee. Now one could wonder how I can compare the sanctity of vaginal comfort to decent coffee, but if you think about it, when you wake up in the morning, what things matter most? The comfort of the vagina, and having a tasty cup of delicious, rich coffee that does not come from a can that reads "Folgers." Aside from world peace and the health and welfare of your loved ones, what could matter more at 6am? Nothing. So, don't go with cheap TP or cheap coffee.

One of the many reasons that my ex-husband is no longer my husband was his lack of concern for those two areas: my vagina, and good coffee.

He seemed to quit caring about the vagina part pretty early on in our relationship, but his utter lack of concern or care of the quality of the coffee, was unforgivable, and eventually written into the "irreconcilable differences" section of our divorce documents.

He mistakenly believed that all coffee was equal. Now, all vaginas might be equal, I have no frame of reference, but I can say unequivocally, all coffee is not the same. Folgers is basically sad, brown water. It's like instant coffee, but it tastes worse. If you, sir or madam, cannot give a damn about the quality of the coffee, I cannot give a damn about you. *(Keep these two factors in mind when seeking a mate or companion; this lesson will take you far).*

Also, don't waste your money on expensive life coaches. Because I think we can all agree that there is really only one thing you need to know about life: DON'T BE AN ASSHOLE. Think about it, that fits pretty much every situation. I'm now your life coach. And saved you thousands of dollars in quasi-therapy, which is what life coaching sessions are when you think about it.

People with more depth than I, may be disappointed to see just two items highlighted in this chapter. It's no secret, I'm a simple woman who knows what she wants. Good coffee, and a comfy vagina. The world is ugly, scary, adventurous and unpredictable. Cling to the things you can control, and things you can afford. I think most of us can afford decent toilet paper and robust coffee. And if not, maybe pick up a little cash by selling weed on the side.

Chapter Seven

DON'T HOLD ONTO PAST RELATIONSHIPS: OR

EXPIRED FOOD

In the long list of things that no one prepared me for as an adult, was the importance of expiration dates. You know what? Regardless of what you see on TV, expiration dates totally matter. Especially when it involves dairy. Ignoring expiration dates is like gambling with a trip down E-Coli Boulevard. *(I have no medical background, I'm just trying to be clever).*

Like expired, fuzzy food at the back of the fridge, expired stuff should get tossed out. Sometimes you have to call in the Haz-Mat team, sometimes you can just hold your nose and stuff it in the can on the curb. During the teen years, humans have this remarkable super power that allows them to successfully ignore, and live peacefully alongside overgrown, fuzzy, toxic food and their containers. That's a disgusting side effect of hormonal overdrive I think, because nothing else explains it. But, I digress!

Relationships have expiration dates too, but they don't hide out in your fridge. They take up valuable space in your life. And make you act like a crazy person. More accurately, I think the crazy already lives inside, but these relationships or perhaps their aftermath, wake up the sleeping crazy.

I hate when I act crazy, but what I really hate is when people I know act crazy. Because it's not enough for them to feel crazy and act crazy -- they have to post cryptic, caustic one-line status updates on Facebook. They post sad, melancholy songs with the lyrics spelled out...for anyone who didn't get the memo that they just got broken up with. Breakups and pain and the side order of crazy that goes with, awaken the Ernest Hemingways and Sylvia Plaths inside. Here's my plea: Keep your crazy in check. Please. Because it's hard to be your friend when you turn everything into a Bryan Adams ballad.

To be clear, break ups suck. They are awful. I have been broken up with. Most of the time, I didn't like it. Everyone reacts to break ups differently. After an acceptable period of mourning or playing really loud music and throwing shit against the wall, you need to accept your new reality. It's over...move on, baby! Like relationships, break ups have expiration dates.

Let's get honest for a minute: the biggest regret of your life is over. Think about it... whatever it is, whoever it is, this shit has already happened. Don't invite that incident, person, or memory to unpack their skanky, stinky laundry and move into your spare room. Not to sound like Dr. Phil *(as if! I don't wear underwear!)*, but you are giving up time that you might not have much of, to focus on shit that already happened. Yep, it might have been like an explosion of awful, but the point is that it's over, Babycakes.

To get bitchy: get over yourself.

I have had a few breakups in my life, I'm actually an excellent breaker-upper. I don't get all dramatic and scream and throw shit. I have been known to totally disappear in fact, which I find to be very unhealthy, but extremely effective. Take for example, when my husband and I decided to get divorced. Extremely lacking in the drama department. It went like this:

"Hey, so how's it going?"

"Meh, pretty good."

"So, do you want to keep doing this, or does it feel like it's run its course?"

"Uh, the second one."

"Right on, so can you move out by the end of the month?"

"Yeah, that sounds about right."

Finite. Done. No drama. And he moved out by the end of the week. We dislike each other more NOW, several years later for some weird reason, than we did during the divorce. The point is, there was really no drama, because we didn't wait until we deeply hated each other to have our break up. So maybe that should be another chapter in this epic non-help novella: don't wait until the hate sets in. Jump ship before bitter comes out to play.

Regrets often have names, like Ron, Andy, Danny, Sheila, Leslie, Amy. Whatever you call your regret, it's time to let those losers fly free and quit controlling your life.

 Clean out your i-pod or digital music player, delete those Bryan Adams ballads and the mushy, squishy songs that make your tear ducts well up. Take the box full of sentimental knick knacks and have a bonfire (if you don't have to get a permit or anything complicated) in the backyard or in your BBQ. Light that shit up, and let it go.

Kinder, more gentle people than I would say things like: remember how great you are, remember how special you are...and you didn't pick this book up for that kind of advice. If you need to create a voodoo doll, do it. Need to burn that bastard in effigy? Do it. But what you can't do, is send them rage texts or light bags of dog poop on their doorstep.

I have been the breaker upper *(I am so good at being a breaker upper!),* and I have been broken up with. And while it might seem like a good idea to take your pain and anger and homicidal rage and give it to the person who deserves it -- wrong.

Here's the thing, for whatever reason, the relationship is done. When you have back and forth with this cretin, no matter how good you think it will make you feel, all you're doing is keeping them in your life. But not the "fun" them. The asshole part of them. Yuck.

I mean think about it. When you were a kid on playground, and some asshole little kid came up to you and kicked you in the shin, did you go running after them and invite them to come back and kick you in the shin some more? Well, kids do weird stuff, so maybe that's a horrible example. But the point is that you need to move forward, and not keep inviting the kick to the shin back into your life.

Once, soon after I got divorced, I was in a really stupid relationship. And stupid doesn't begin to cover it. There was nothing that we had in common aside from electrifying chemistry. Without that, we probably would have hated each other, and sometimes we did. We were addicted to the chaos and the sex.

We would break up and then the break up wouldn't take. It would be "off" for about 10 days and then one of us couldn't take the withdrawal, and suddenly we would be right back to our chaotic, sexual relationship. Which felt better than being lonely and reminiscing. At least for a little bit, until we spent time together and remembered why we broke up in the first place. We didn't really like each other.

Like any confused teenager living in an adult body, I stayed in this ridiculous spiral for about 18 months longer than I should have. Not my proudest achievement. But I learned from the battle scars. I quit playing our songs. I quit looking at pictures. I quit talking about him. I quit texting him and quit taking his calls. I also quit getting laid, and truthfully that was the most disappointing part.

So, it hurts, but you already took the sucker punch. Your strongly worded, clever text (which is never as clever as you think), isn't going to give you finality or closure. It's going to invite an equally strong response, and remind you why this person is a dick. You might feel righteous or justified for a few minutes, but you'll just keep chasing that dragon. Put down the crack pipe, babe. It's only in movies that shit works out exactly like you thought. Everything else is just real life, and sometimes real life is a kick to the crotch.

If you're trying to get through a break-up, you have to do what you have to do. It's totally legit to allow yourself a few days to cry and scream and lay around and pout. I know I sound more and more like a girl every time I say something like that. But I think we're all allowed to break down for a little while. Take that pint of ice cream to the bedroom, wash it down with some vodka, and grab the remote. Fall apart for a few days, but keep the phone away from you. Don't text them, call them, or look through pictures of them on your phone.

There are experts who would strongly disagree with my "leave 'em in the dirt pile you found them in" approach, and you can find their book in the self-help section. That's not where this book lives, and it's not my style.

If I wasn't clear, I'm not very sensitive. And it's not my job to make you feel better, I'm just trying to stop you from doing stupid stuff. When food gets old and stinky you toss it, when people and relationships get stinky you get to do the same thing.

Chapter Eight

DON'T ASSUME FAMOUS PEOPLE ARE COOL

Seriously. When I'm at the dentist office or at my kid's 300th orthodontist appointment, I leaf through magazines. I see those stupid "Who's Hot & Who's Not" lists. Which are never accurate, by the way. Celebrities are just like the rest of us. But worse.

I can speak from some authority, lest you forget, being propositioned by a washed-up rock star. But that perv wasn't the only famous person I ran into. I guess I'm blessed in that way. Not that I'm a name dropper. But...

You know that guy from that one group? The red headed guy who sings in Metallica? That guy. Well once upon a time, my teenage daughter and I were at an all-day music festival in the San Francisco Bay Area. My daughter, being a girl, and a teenager, was emphatically telling me a story. As she was getting more into the part of the story where she was telling someone to "go fuck themselves," up pulls a black Escalade with tinted windows.

Neither of us were paying much attention as the Escalade pulled up in front of us. The window rolled down and I noticed the red headed passenger, watching my daughter intently, mid-meltdown. She turned his direction, their eyes locked, and as she emphatically repeated "fuck you!" it dawned on me who she accidentally told to fuck off. That red headed dude from Metallica! Who was laughing his ass off. I'm pretty sure he has daughters.

See? Celebrities are just like us. And sometimes they are worse. Which you find out when you fly Southwest. Where all the D-list celebrities fly.

I was on my way to Nashville, via Los Angeles, because if you're in Northern California it's damn near impossible to get a direct flight to anywhere, ever. The flight to Los Angeles was overbooked and we were crammed in like sardines. Again, flying Southwest is generally a shit show, so you probably knew that already.

I boarded the flight headed for Nashville and was expecting another cramped, oversold, long ass flight to Tennessee. From the West Coast it takes about 4.5 hours to get to the Bible Belt. Ironically enough, I was going to the Bible Belt to get really drunk and hang out on a boat with my friends. Irony is fun! But back to my flight...

I grabbed the first empty seat I saw, which happened to be a middle seat and the window seat was occupied.

I make it a rule to never, ever speak to strangers. I cannot recall one time in my life when talking to a stranger ever worked out well. With this as my mantra, you can imagine that I had zero intention of even looking to my left to notice the guy wearing a baseball hat and knock off Raybans.

Ok, I only noticed because he looked like the Unabomber but without the hoodie. Turns out he wasn't the actual Unabomber, but one has to be careful. You can't trust TSA to catch them all.

I buckled up and pulled out the i-pod, when I got a tap-tap-tap on my shoulder.

"You know this isn't a sold-out flight, right?"

I looked around and noticed empty seats all around. It took me a slow let-go-my-ego second to realize what he was really saying. He was saying, "get the hell away from me."

I'm generally the one who offends and insults others, I don't take it well when it's flung my direction. What a douche.

"You know I wasn't trying to sit next to you, right?" I was all up in the indignant zone when I flung myself into the aisle seat. I made sure to give a disapproving glare to Passenger Dick, just so I'd feel

better. I still wasn't sure what he looked like, but the Raybans inside the plane were definitely a dick move. I was annoyed that I'd have to be in an uppity mood for the next four hours, but he started it. And it was on.

I am very skilled at "cold shouldering." I've discovered that it can make even the most D list celebrity uncomfortable. We'd been in the air for about 20 minutes when I felt tap-tap-tap on my shoulder again.

"You want to see our latest video?"

Video? The invisible man, two seats away, didn't want my *accidental* attention. Suddenly, he wanted my intentional attention. FUCK THAT.

I have never met a person who could be more vindictive and less forgiving than, well, me. Over really petty stuff, if that wasn't clear. But I also believe "to thine own self be true," which shows a certain kind of strength, don't you think?

In ice queen mode, I barely acknowledged my fellow passenger, but he persisted, and eventually I sighed heavily, did a dramatic head tilt, and allowed him to show me his video. Which is when it hit me. I was finally certain of who this D Lister was. And guess what? I still didn't want to sit next to him. And in my pettiness, I really needed him to know that I didn't care for him. Not one bit.

When I commit to acting like a bitch, I commit 110%, so I kept pretending not to know who he was. I did know, but I would not let on.

I was in Seattle once, walking in downtown with my then 8-year-old daughter. There was a marquee that said "Evan & Jaron" outside The Showbox theatre. I had no idea if this was a movie, an art show, a lecture...but my squealing 8-year-old knew exactly who Evan & Jaron were. She proceeded to sing the pop sugary song that had made this pair of 20 something twins famous.

Since I never listened to Top 40 radio, I was totally ignorant to their charm. But I did enjoy my daughter's impromptu street performance, so I looked them up when I got home.

Meh. Sugary. Sweet. Poppy.

After an appropriate amount of time passed, I said, *"Hey, didn't you and your brother **used to be** famous?"* This seemed to irritate him, which was the entire point. Back in the day, he and his brother were cute, they sang in sweet harmony, but I believe their records only sold because they were cute, and 12-year-old girls get allowance. *(You can Google "Crazy for This Girl" if you want a glimpse of the one hit wonders).*

Because the cheap air travel gods are cruel, I was seated next to this almost celebrity with an over inflated sense of self. And he was pretty much as arrogant as any really good looking D list celebrity could be.

Believe it or not, by the end of the flight, this guy who originally couldn't wait for me to remove my vile self, was trying to look down my shirt and asking what my plans were in Nashville. Listen, I'm not saying I'm a hottie, because I'm not. I don't think I'm special, but I don't think very many people are special. What I'm saying is, celebrities are pretty much just like everyone else. Sometimes worse.

But lest you think that I only run into pervy (little guy from Hall & Oates), charming (Metallica guy), or sketchy (Evan or Jaron, I can't be sure), I also run into vile, gross, and thankfully now dead, famous people.

There is a crazy little "church" in the mid-west, made up of family members (I would have said inbred, but I can't say that with any accuracy). Until recently, they were led by this crazy looking, always screaming, down right hateful old guy who would hold up charming signs like "God Hates Fags." I'm sure you've probably heard of them.

Believe it or not, there was a time in my life when I had no idea who these charming people were. But that all changed when I was in Golden Gate Park, participating in the AIDS Walk, proudly waddling next to my 9-year-old and our family friend. I was waddling because I was pregnant, but true zealots don't care if you have a swollen belly and a small child beside you.

What they really care about is yelling at you about how AIDS is God's wrath and how "Fag Enablers Burn in Hell." Charming, right? Especially charming when you're participating in an event meant to help bring awareness and monies to a global cause. With your child.

My daughter recoiled in terror and hid behind me, while my friend and I pushed passed the dick with the sandwich board sign. His spittle landed on all 3 of us, no one could accuse him of being frail. It turns out, the guy I mistook for an angry dementia patient who'd broken loose from his mental health ward, was the leader of this insane sect of lunatics who were famous.

I yelled to my daughter, *"Hey, remember that crazy old man who spit at us today? Come look, he's on the news!"* We didn't make it on the news, but we learned that wherever this crazy guy went, with his hateful signs, he made headlines.

Now that he's dead, I can only wonder...how many other people did this lunatic spit on that day? How many small children had he terrified in his pathetic lifetime? I'm certain the number is staggering, and yet I still like the thought of me and my family being in an exclusive club: **I got spit on by the old angry guy from that church** club. It would be cool to get together and share stories about what sign he was holding when he spat upon us.

So, listen up, don't believe that someone's status makes them any better than you. People suck everywhere you go, my friend. Celebrity or not.

Chapter Nine

DON'T BELIEVE THE LIES BROWN LIQUOR TELLS YOU

I know, the biggest lies come wrapped in the prettiest packages. I've been there. I've also been on the bathroom floor, not only the next morning, but sometimes while out with friends, supposedly "enjoying" my liquor. Those are nights when unforgettable memories are forged. On the verge of passing out, while on the toilet (literally), pants on the ground, upper body blocking the stall door, whimpering to a co-worker to help you. Now that is one pretty picture, am I right?

As the night goes on and your co-worker is forced to crawl under the bathroom stall door to rescue you, it just gets more and more horrifying. Or so I have heard.

In my twenties, when getting carded would make me giggle, I couldn't spend my paycheck fast enough at those Thursday night after-work deals, where people I barely knew got all chummy and silently judged who could drink the most. The winner was treated like some sort of champion the next day, back slapping, exaggerated laughter, and a general fake camaraderie. And yet every week, I threw my hat in the ring, and my paycheck into the gutter, consuming ridiculous amounts of brown liquor.

Why did I do this, week after week? It could have been due to the fact that I didn't get enough positive attention as a child, it could have been a ridiculous desire to fit in, or more likely, it was my competitive nature. Maybe someone double dog dared me, but I would drink as hard as I could, so I could win the respect of co-workers I didn't even like.

I have friends who are connoisseur of tequilas. They can tell you which is the best tequila, which tequila is hand crafted in which charming village, and the exact history of what I call "devil's blood."

As a grown up, I've come to understand that tequila is meant to be sipped. Too bad my adult self couldn't tell my twenties self that liquor could be sipped. Apparently, it's not a pre-requisite that it gets slammed down the gullet from a tiny shot glass. Some lessons don't really take until after they have punched you in the face.

I shouldn't just pick on tequila. Dark liquors typically ruin my life, or at least my week. Being immature and having a competitive nature, and the ability to purchase alcohol legally, can be a dangerous concoction of bad ideas and fate.

More times than I can count, my cocky self would feel the need to participate in stupid things like "drinking contests." Generally, I'd only participate in these contests if I was sure it would be a challenge. Often, I reflect on my life and wonder how I get by without a full-time handler or nurse.

Perhaps worse than tequila would be the devil juice called Jägermeister. This stuff doesn't even try to taste good. It tastes just like the cough medicine that your mom used to force down your throat while you tried not to gag. Jägermeister also cost about $6 per shot, and smells like something died in the bottle. What's not to love?

Here are just a few of the lies brown liquor has told me:

- You can totally pull off that outfit

- He was *sooooo* flirting with you

- That was super clever. Repeat it, several times, but louder

- No one saw that

- You can totally have another, it will be fine

- These people are *loving* your story

- The bathroom floor isn't that bad

- No one will even remember what you did

- People really like you, they really like you

- You're totally going to win this drinking contest

All lies. Fuck you, brown liquor!

What no one ever told me (being a woman) was that when a man invites you (or in my case, double dog dares you) to participate in any kind of drinking contest, it's generally because they want to get into your pants. Lucky for me, alcohol would take over, barfing would kick in, and that would kill any kind of sexual vibe my sexy self was spinning. I think once the barfing starts, you can light the Bat signal – the night is over, my friends.

In all seriousness, times have changed and some people become predatory when they have access to someone who has overindulged. That's a truly troubling thing and I don't make light of it. Consent is #1.

Back when I was a drinking way too much and making dangerous choices, trust me, vomiting really did act like a safety net. The hangover was the price you paid, but you were otherwise safe.

In my dimly lit world view, I didn't put the pieces together that I had never won a single drinking contest, and yet with one "double dog dare" I'd be in for a horrible night, much worse morning, and definitely embarrass myself. Turns out I am not that great a dancer, I've got zero volume control when doing anything drunk, and eventually I tell everyone that I'm deeply in love with them. Everyone. I am grateful every day that when I was young and stupid, there was no such thing as You Tube and people didn't carry little digital cameras in their pockets.

What did I learn from my ill-fated drinking contests? 1) Liquor goes down quickly, and when it comes up, it doesn't stop 2) It tastes better on the way down 3) Stomach acid can and will strip away the paint on a car door. Valuable lessons. I invested many horrible nights learning these lessons in my twenties so I could stop doing stupid stuff like that.

Seriously, this is what's known as a life hack: if you or someone you are travelling with ends up accidently vomiting the entirety of their stomach contents all over a car door, it's of vital importance to get that car door to an all-night car wash as fast as humanly possible.

It will be extremely important to use industrial strength soap and really scrub off the barf. The diligent scrubbing cannot be stressed enough, if you don't want to end up buying a car door from the pick-n-pull lot. Not only do you have to pay for the door, but you also have to pay a professional to install the new door. At least that's how I remember it. And I have barfed on more than one car door.   It gets pricey!

Moral of the chapter: liquor doesn't make everything better. I do my fair share of day drinking, and night drinking, and going to bars, and parties. But years of waking up in strange places with funny signs taped to my head taught me that double dog dares rarely end well for me, and liquor is a fucking liar.

Chapter Ten

DON'T PUT ALL YOUR DRAMA ON SOCIAL MEDIA

First, let's assume that you're not 17 years old. That being said, nobody wants to read your drama on Facebook. Nothing says "I'm an adult" like spilling intimate life details in a cryptic one or two sentence status update. Be honest...tell me you don't roll your eyes when you see that shit.

For the love of all that is holy and what-not, part of being an adult is recognizing that sometimes life sucks. And is unfair. And bad shit happens. Recall the chapter discussing how crappy break ups are. Life can get yucky.

Your friends and mine, do not need to learn about the break-up of your marriage, or the arrest of your stupid sister, or the devastation of your bankruptcy...on Facebook. If I wanted to be shocked and awed and horrified at how awful human beings are, I could simply log onto Twitter for about 3 minutes.

Ever since the 2016 Presidential election, you need only look at the insults, banality, and insanity that come from the Tweeter in Chief, to be reminded how social media in the wrong hands is a fucking nightmare. I never thought I'd be talking about "that" guy, but hey, he is an excellent example of what not to do.

Facebook is a delicate balance, because you also don't want to be that motivational, sappy, touchy feely, "let me uplift you" person either. Constantly sharing motivational memes and quotes from Marianne Williamson make you seem just as vapid as the person who overshares everything.

I'm not the social media police, and yes, I am super judgmental. If that sort of thing really irritated you, you'd never have made it this far into the book. So, hang in there a little longer. I am only going to be annoying for another several pages.

I keep my Facebook circle small, and I unfollow the hell out of people during election cycles and world disasters. Not because I'm an asshole, but because after I've seen which side of the debate you're on...I get it. I don't need more. You're either right, or you're not, but once I figure out who you are, I'm good.

I think technology has bred not only cyber bullying, and possibly addictions to pornography, but it has most definitely emboldened us to say whatever the fuck we want, damn the consequences. Not sure this is a good thing.

What I do like about Facebook is seeing pictures of your dog (cute cats are totally acceptable, too), your baby (let's not get crazy, one or two every week is fine), and if you're making your relationship "Facebook official" I will probably give the status a "thumbs up." I don't know that I really care all that much, but I know it spreads good will and good cheer, so what the hell? Congrats on finding another human who likes you enough to tell people!

However, when that relationship ends, I don't think it's necessary to tell all of us. Truth be told, most of Facebook isn't all that invested in your relationship. Just slink into a bottle of liquor and a tub of ice cream for a few days, and silently remove the pictures of your former lover from your profile. The rest of the world probably won't notice.

Facebook is much more enjoyable when I don't have to give "thumbs up" to status updates like "Bob is now single." Those updates seem awkward. It would be just as awkward in person, but most people don't just blurt out "I'm single now!" Unless we're talking about social media.

I think technology in general is not the proper venue for making big announcements. Maybe "I got the job!" or "I can't make it, I have e-coli!" are OK, but beyond that maybe a phone call, an invitation or announcement through the mail, or in person conversation might be better when sharing the big stuff.

Imagine my surprise to learn that my 19-year-old daughter had gotten married – via a text message. Allow me to stroll down memory lane and paint a picture. I was on vacation with friends in Tennessee (that phase of my life is over, I rarely travel to Tennessee anymore, but still love moonshine), driving to a child's beauty pageant of all things. Child beauty pageants are big in the South, and should be avoided at all costs. But I digress...

While I was riding in a car, pummeling through the back roads of Alabama, a text came through on my phone. It was from my daughter. I opened it to find a picture of some freaky looking kid with streaked hair, leaning against a beater car. The message said: "Meet your new son-in-law." Luckily for everyone in the car, I wasn't driving.

It probably wasn't wise for my 19-year-old to marry an almost stranger, she had met on the internet, while her mom was across the country. It definitely wasn't wise to announce this glorious news via text message. I don't know if you know this about me, but I don't handle surprises well.

The ride home from the airport was a bit awkward, seeing as how my newlywed daughter was the one driving me home. But that's just how life goes sometimes with daughters. Everyone survived, the husband was a total weirdo as his picture suggested, there was an eventual divorce, and we all survived.

I can say in all honesty, that I drank more moonshine on that vacation than was probably wise. And a simple phone call BEFORE the impromptu wedding might have been good, although I still would have drunk too much moonshine.

The moral of the story is: save the big announcement for phone calls, in person visits, or beautifully designed mailers. Don't post your personal shit on Facebook. Your friends totally support this message, even if they haven't told you.

Chapter Eleven

DON'T MAKE EYE CONTACT WITH THE NEIGHBORS

You may recall that I have a policy that forbids me from interacting with strangers. It's for the safety and comfort of everyone. Some people think of strangers as "friends you just haven't met yet." That is complete and utter bullshit. Strangers are strange, and there is a reason you don't know them.

I believe I have mentioned previously that I am not turned off by pornography, and I've certainly watched my fair share, thanks to the internet. I know lots of women are uncomfortable with pornography, or rather, admitting that they watch it. Most of my female friends pretend it doesn't exist, or at the very least, refuse to talk about it.

I get it. I was raised Roman Catholic and I am very familiar with guilt and the foils of sexual awareness, and dare I say it...sexual activity. Damn it all to hell!

This is a religion that told me as a child that I could easily go blind if I, gasp, masturbated. Can you imagine my horror in being told as a child that I needed glasses?

Yikes, the priest was right! I needed glasses because I was a secret masturbater, and it wasn't a secret anymore! My glasses were worse than a scarlet letter. People were going to look at me and say, *"See, she masturbated, and look what happened...she almost went blind!"*

Now that was one fun religion! And another reason I'm not a practicing Catholic. Also, weekly services and Lent.

However, since I've painted the picture for you, I bet the next person you see with glasses – you're going to peg them as a secret masturbater! Mission accomplished. Just kidding. Everyone masturbates, glasses or not.

One of the lessons I learned from pornography is LIFE IS NOT A PORN MOVIE. I say that, because it might put this chapter in better context. It also may get you to finally throw this book into the trash. Either way...

Because I recognized pornography as fantasy, I was ill prepared for the oddly disproportionate number of times I was propositioned to participate in threesomes. Seriously. In pornos, a threesome is basically just a regular Tuesday, but for me, it was just something that happened in porn clips, and with old flailing rock stars *(thanks for ruining my innocence, Mr. Oates!).*

I walk around the world without a full-time handler or nurse, as I've mentioned previously. So, I am often ill prepared for the weird stuff that happens to me. People are just strange, there is no getting around it.

This is probably an appropriate time to comment on pornography. It feels like I make mention of pornography a lot. I do not actually consume pornography as often as it probably sounds. In the event that this book lands in the hand of my children, it just seems important to point that out. As it could fall into the hands of my future mate, I should probably mention it as well, so as to keep expectations realistic.

That being said, I am very judgmental with most things, but I am absolutely not judgey about people's sex lives. I actually root for people who have active sex lives. Part of that might be jealousy, part of that might be amazement, but trust that if you're having sex, I'm rooting for you! I don't feel the need to be there in person with pom poms however, in case you were going to ask.

As an average looking woman, who is absolutely not friendly to strangers, I have no idea how in the hell I've been asked to join so many couples in their bedrooms. I think most adults may run into that situation once or twice in their lifetimes. I'm up to 8.

Actually, it's rarely been strangers...it starts with the neighbors. When I was in my twenties I lived in an apartment complex full of colorful people. Nothing as exciting as Melrose Place, but enough people to make me run from the car to my front door every time I came home.

For a short period of time, I had a roommate. She was crazy, of course. I think that's a pre-requisite with a roommate, isn't it? She was a friend of my weed selling brother, whom I was still speaking to at the time. I blame him for introducing me to this nut case. But, I digress...

Lori moved in to help me offset the rent and she liked to drink and smoke weed, and in my twenties that was actually a stamp of approval. So, I probably played a part in the disaster, but this isn't about me taking responsibility for my life, it's about telling you how crazy people can be.

She would disappear for long periods of time, sometimes a day or two, and then meander back home, no mention of where she had been or who she had been doing. Apparently, she had been doing the neighbors.

These days were pre-internet, so I was still a little fuzzy on porn, and I didn't know that your neighbors could be swingers. Looking back, I can't be sure I knew what the term "swinger" actually meant.

I had heard about "Key Parties" from the 70s. Couples would drop their set of keys into a bowl at the party, and whether randomly or by design, they would select a set of keys and through that decision, sexual partners would be exchanged. In that context, I understood what swinging was.

Again, no judgements, but it had always been uncomfortable for me when the invitations got extended, and there have been far too many invitations for my comfort. In this particular case, adding to the awkwardness was that these neighbors were extremely unattractive.

Lori took off for a weekend and the neighbor came by my apartment looking for her. When I told him that she was gone, he made up some excuse to get me over to his apartment, probably something stupid like, "Hey, my wife wanted to ask you something."

Like the rookie that I was, I took it to mean that my neighbor's wife, also my neighbor, wanted to ask me something. When I got to the apartment she opened the door wearing a terry cloth bathrobe and a stupid smile.

There is nothing sexy about a terry cloth bathrobe, I think the world agrees. When you're going to be getting sexed up, I think the preferred wardrobe is silky or maybe nothing at all. But here she was in her terry cloth robe and that didn't raise my suspicions.

I knew she was a mom and assumed her kid was home. Oops.

As I walked into the apartment, her husband slipped in behind me, and I heard music from the stereo, and almost choked on the cigarette smoke. To cut to the chase, the undignified, horrifying invitation came a few minutes later when the couple asked me if I knew what Lori did when she came over to visit them.

I just assumed Lori went over to their apartment to get high, which she did an awful lot. Turns out it was way more than getting high, it was getting naked and banging the neighbors.

I am absolutely awkward around people I know well, people I actually like, people who are fully dressed and don't want to have sex with me. Imagine how awkward I am around strangers who want to bang me. It really doesn't get much worse.

I couldn't stop myself from screeching, "Holy crap! No way, you guys are gross!" I sprinted from their apartment as fast as I could and knew immediately that I had to move.

Did I mention they were very unattractive? And I was still not even 100% sure what happened in a threesome. But I knew I didn't want to see either one of them naked. Plus, they were my neighbors! Gah, pack up the U-Haul and hit the road!

But lest you think it's just quasi-strangers that have invited me into their bedrooms, it has also happened with life-long friends.

Which is somehow worse. Who would assume that a birthday party for a 10-year-old would lead to a proposition? Not me, that's who!

Being a rookie at life can be challenging. I thought nothing of my girlfriend asking me to come keep her company while she held a sleepover birthday party for her 10-year-old. I envisioned us drinking wine and checking on the kids from time to time. I did not envision her husband propositioning me.

After the guests, and by guests, I mean 10-year-old girls, had arrived, my friend's husband said, "Hey, let's go grab a beer!" It's rare that I turn down the offer to get a beer. I knew this couple as friends and one-time co-workers, so to me, a beer was just a beer.

Once at the pub, the beers arrived and my friend's husband looked at me and said:

"So, I hear you're going through something of a dry spell."

"What's that, now?"

"Yeah, Michelle says you haven't had a boyfriend in a while."

"I guess not, but..."

"Well, Michelle and I were talking, and there's no easy way to ask this, but..."

(shivers)

"Ok, ask me what?"

"How would you feel about waking up to breakfast with us tomorrow?"

"Like sleepover? I mean, I guess. Do you think the kids will really be that wild? You need reinforcement?"

"Uh, no. I'm asking if you want to sleepover...with us. In our room."

"Oh, for fuck sake."

Why can't a beer with your friend's husband just be a beer with your friend's husband? I mean, I don't understand people. Obviously, I turned him down. And that was the most awkward ride back to the house to pick up my car. Did I mention I was probably going to see them at work on Monday?

That friendship took a quick jump off the *"fuck this, it's over!"* bridge, and I still had to see them at work, dressed up and professional. All the while I was thinking, you cheeky fuckers. I had to get a new job.

Sadly, for me, and countless other couples, this was not the last time I'd turn down offers of big love. I have never been able to put my finger on the attraction couples have towards me. I barely catch the attention of the guy in the produce section. But apparently, I'm a magnet for horny couples.

Because of the silly number of times that I've been invited to join couples in their bedroom activities, I've discovered that I really cannot be friends with couples. Seriously. I can be friends with the boyfriend or husband, most of my friends are male. There's a possibility I could get along with the wife or girlfriend. I cannot however be friends with the couple. I have to choose one or the other. I don't know if there is a name for this syndrome, but I definitely have it!

The moral of the story is: do what you want, do who you want, but please don't invite me in on it. Also, be careful about making eye contact with the neighbors. You don't want to give them the wrong idea.

Chapter Twelve

DON'T BE "THAT" PARENT: YOU'LL SCREW THEM UP

I'm not a life coach, therapist, or even a "woke" person – as the kids say nowadays. But I am a parent of two humans, and I have some stuff I need to say. Because if your kids are out in the world and screwed up, they might screw up my kids. Nobody wants that!

There are some things in this world that are universally true, and this is one: if you are an idiot parent, you're going to mess up your kids. Also, mean people make little mean people. So, stop it.

Screwing up your kids sort of creeps up on you. No one ever plans to screw up their kids. I know this from experience, because I have done some really stupid things to my own. Not on purpose, but because I have zero filter and say whatever comes into my mind, if that wasn't clear by now.

I have done a lot of things in my life that were not on purpose, not accidents per say, but things that just sort of happened. I became a parent that way. To be clear, my kid was not an accident. I just didn't plan it out.

I never **planned** to say:

"You're going to wear that?!"

"That's the dumbest thing I've ever heard."

"Wait until I tell your Dad."

"I don't even know who you are anymore."

"That bathing suit is not a good idea."

"Is that really the best you can do?"

"What, are you depressed again?"

How's that for being a total idiot parent? I've said all of those things and about 1000 more things that really upset the kiddos. Fortunately, my daughters still speak to me, but probably, mostly because I never whooped them.

If you were a child in the 60s or 70s, you probably remember the dreaded wooden spoon. My mother had one to use in the kitchen, the other was tucked into her purse at all times. If my brother or I acted out, the wooden spoon came out, and we would be beaten within an inch of our lives...right there in public. Nobody cared. I'm pretty sure people didn't even notice. There were children all across the Mall getting their whacks in, and it didn't raise a single eyebrow.

We also didn't wear seatbelts. I can remember sitting in the back of the neighbor's station wagon, careening about the back, head hitting the roof of the car as we sped down the highway. It was such a freeing time.

Not so great for kids if you didn't want to die. No seatbelts, whacks to the head with wooden spoons, and sometimes even a good smack across the face if you got lippy.

When I became a parent, I knew the 70s were over. We didn't whack our kids anymore, and we buckled them into the car, sometimes even using booster seats until they were well into the third grade. Sometimes the safety rules seem over the top, but most would agree it's a good thing that walls aren't covered in lead paint anymore. The pendulum had swung back, way back, since the fun filled days of my childhood. I had learned from the mistakes of those who came before me. That was the easy stuff. Duh.

Today, we don't beat on our kids. But we do beat them down. By trying to help them fit in, by trying to get them the best grade in class, by trying to make sure they don't stand out. Fuck that. Help your kid stand out and be different.

Walk with me down memory lane for a moment. In 1994, the world lost Kurt Cobain. While I subscribe to the theory that his crazy wife helped off him, most of the world might recall that the lead singer of Nirvana died in his home in Seattle, suicide or not.

I for one, have never bought the suicide story. Kurt could never have dosed himself with that amount of heroin, written the ridiculous suicide note, held a shotgun at that bizarre angle, cleaned up his fix-it kit, and still pulled the trigger. But, the point is...for whatever reason, this dead man became very important to my daughter, who was born in 1992.

Trying to help my daughter fit in, I enrolled her in the dreaded Girl Scouts brigade. What could be better than baking and hiking and learning to be a good citizen, while earning badges and hawking really gross cookies? Nothing! We lived in suburbia!

Well, said kid wasn't one to fit in. And I didn't always appreciate how awesome not fitting in could be. She was creative, and loud, and sweet, and cried when she saw homeless people. She would see the drought-stricken hills of California, and want to find a way to water them. This kid had the heart of a lion.

Surely my musical and cultural interest seeped into my kid's awareness. She became very interested in Kurt Cobain, his music, his lyrics, and his death. I didn't mean to infect her with my stuff, but it happens.

So, when the Girl Scouts had a talent show, while the other kids took the stage and showed off their singing, their hula hooping, and their dance moves, my daughter read a heart -felt ode she had written about Kurt Cobain.

 I am 100% sure that not one mother at that talent show had any idea who Kurt was, and none of their Girl Scouts did either. It was one of the proudest moments of my life, listening to my 8-year-old pay homage to the dead guy.

I knew then that it was more important to stoke the fires of creativity and uniqueness, than it was to help her fit in. What did it mean to fit in, anyway? Trying to fit in would mean bending to other people's ideals and images about life. Well, that wasn't going to work. And I didn't want it to.

Was that a defining moment in my daughter's life? She has had so many epic moments of uniqueness and creativity, it might be an almost forgotten memory. For me, it was my "coming out" moment as a parent. I did not want to raise a kid who felt the need to conform.

Recently, a pretty wise person told me that he had a theory about adulthood. He thought most people lived in a FOG.

- F for Fear

- O for Obligation

- G for Guilt

I recognized that as a universal truth, and was grateful that I didn't live there.

Not that I was the pillar of motherhood. I did try to get the tattoo shop to give my daughter the tatt she wanted when she was 15. Why not? I didn't blink an eye when my youngest asked if she could shave half of her head. It's just hair! It grows back! Plus, it sort of miffed her father and that was a bonus.

When I was about 16 years old, my friends and I had this brilliant idea to cut class, steal some beer from one of the dads, and drive to the park...the park about a block from our high school, and day drink, right there in public. So much stupidity with the plan, you could pretty much take any part of that story and see where things took a turn.

The stealing the beer part went smoothly, but when we reached the park and started to stumble out of the car, a couple of the bottles broke on the asphalt, sending us into fits of laughter. We choked the beers down, we didn't really like beer, of course...and then headed back to school.

Whether it was us bragging to classmates, or acting stupid(er) at school, somehow word got back to our parents that we weren't where we were supposed to be and severe punishments were doled out. Some of us got punished more harshly than others. Pretty sure I got the wooden spoon and then some.

As a parent, how would I have handled that situation? I would not have beat the crap out of my kid. What I did do was kill her with kindness the next morning, when she was cursing life itself with her first, and probably worst hangover of her young life. As I poured her some coffee and spoke to her in hushed tones, my daughter asked me, *"Mom, why are you being so nice to me? When is the punishment coming?"*

I told her that the pain from the hangover definitely trumped any punishment I could dole out. And I meant it – there was nothing I could do to her that would make her feel any worse, she was already pretty close to death.

In no way do I think I'm the "cool" mom, or even a good parent most of the time...but I have learned that life itself sometimes hands out its own consequences. Your kids will figure some shit out, all on their own. Be their safety net, but don't shame them. Or beat them with wooden spoons.

I have screwed up so many times in my life, and most of the time it didn't matter. Where I'd like to think it matters is that my kids know they can be themselves, they can get the grades they get, they can listen to the music they want, they can have the hair that makes them happy.

Don't make your kids crazy with your insecurities. Honestly, bend the rules once in a while. Your kids aren't here to correct your mistakes, and they aren't here to live out your dreams. So, let them shave their heads and get the tatts. Just saying!

Chapter Thirteen

DON'T TELL ME TO CALM DOWN

Think of a time in your life when someone telling you to "calm down" was actually helpful. Did you calm down? Or did you want to punch them in the throat? That's my point. When someone is freaked out, crying, screaming, or in melt down mode, the most patronizing and dangerous thing you could say to them is "calm down."

I am known for handling my business. Not in a street thug sort of way, but in the every day, soccer mom, yoga pants wearing, latte sipping kind of way...I don't get rattled easily. So, if you see me losing my shit, there are two obvious choices: back away slowly, or tell me to calm down. Guess what 9 out of 10 medical professionals recommend?

If you've read previous chapters, you know that I held many different careers. One in particular was at a zoo. In the interest of the general public, and myself, I did have limited access to animals that could eat humans. But, we did experience a handful of crisis situations, which had to be downplayed or hidden from the public. Until today! The scandals! I'll risk telling you, because we're almost friends.

The mom down the street would not take their kiddos to the zoo if they understood physics. Physics would tell you that it isn't all that difficult for the lioness to scale the fence. It's not too far out of reach to imagine the elephant rushing the fence and running rampant throughout the zoo, squashing everything in sight.

I'm not saying these things happen, although one of those two *did* actually happen when I worked at the zoo. What I can tell you is that the one phrase never broadcast on the employee radio: "calm down." Why? Because "calm down" never helped anyone! And for fuck sake, we had a lioness loose in the zoo!

Most people won't find themselves faced with the prospect of an African lion stalking them or small children, so maybe that wasn't the most relatable example. However, most people have computers in their homes, and those can create a threat too. Not the "run for your life, you could get mauled" type of threat, but a threat to your suburban serenity type of threat.

Several years ago, when I was married, my ex-husband worked shift work and we kept very different schedules. You may recall that good coffee and vaginas weren't really his thing. But he was a fan of drinking lots of cheap beer, smoking lots of cigarettes, and parking himself in front of his computer, late at night, while the rest of the house was sleeping.

This particular evening, the husband called me from his job and asked me to make sure that the email he was supposed to send to his lawyer (the first wife was a lot of fun, taking us to court every 3 weeks!) had gone through. Working for large corporation, he wasn't supposed to log onto his work computer for anything non-business related. Too bad for him, really.

He gave me his password (dummy!) and as soon as I logged on, I was greeted with about 5 chat windows, all messages waiting for his responses. Oops.

I am not a person who snoops. I don't go through people's drawers, personal papers, or their phones. I'm not suspicious by nature, and maybe that has to do with my general lack of interest in how other people are living their lives, including my spouse. He clearly had lost interest in how I was living my life, as well.

Looking back, I can chuckle at reading sexual messages from women across the country, sent to one of the least sexual people I knew, the one I was married to. At the time I wasn't really laughing, I was overwhelmed by nausea. SexySunshine2000 called him "Baby" and said she missed him. YoursForeva18 couldn't sleep because she was imagining his hands on her body. Oh, ladies...you've no idea.

The one thing that my husband did not say to me, when I told him that SexySunshine was missing him, was "calm down." If I remember correctly he actually grunted and then hung up on me. Instead of calming down, I took great delight in sending these lovely ladies heart felt messages from the wife.

It was important to me that they knew who they were actually talking to, and it wasn't a super hot single guy. Turns out most of these women didn't care. I'm not sure they were actually women themselves, which was neither here nor there. I didn't think too much of them, of the idiot they were talking to, over internet chat. I was calm, vindictive, and focused.

The next step in not calming down involved changing his password to "Lying_Bastard," and I am not making that up. My sexy husband would have to figure out another way to tantalize his stable of sexy fillies. Because his Yahoo account no longer belonged to him.

When I shared my epic discovery with my friends, they didn't tell me to calm down. Because I was calm, I was diabolical, and I had the password. Oh, the internet! So much fun! And I was calm the whole time. The "let's split up" conversation happened a few months later, but it definitely wasn't because of the internet chat.

It was more about the vagina and the coffee thing.

Telling someone who is not calm, to "calm down," is sort of like telling your teenage daughter, who is bereft and crying from a broken heart, to "suck it up," or "stop crying." Because that always works so well.

It's as bad as telling someone who is having a really bad day, "just smile." Um, how about I just punch you in your face? That might make me smile. Or when you're depressed and can't get out of bed, and your friends say, "get over it," or "take some vitamins," or "exercise." Empty platitudes are patronizing and make people hate you. And no one has ever felt better by smiling or taking vitamins!

As someone who offends people regularly, I know from experience what most people get upset by. I have said "fuck you" to almost everyone I have ever met. But you know what upset them more than that? When I said "calm down." For your safety, my sanity, and the good of humanity...don't tell people to calm down. They'd prefer you told them to fuck off.

Chapter Fourteen

DON'T BELIEVE EVERYTHING YOU READ

A good rule of thumb is not to believe everything you read, and not just on the internet. It applies to pretty much everything, including this book.

Listen, if I mentioned something that happened to me, here in these pages, it definitely happened. I have no shame, I'm not embarrassed at my faux paus. Maybe someone will learn something from them, or at least my friends will have new things to laugh about behind my back.

My point is, nobody is an expert on your life, except for you. Even in those moments when you have absolutely no idea what the hell you're doing...you sort of do know what you're doing. Own it, and be proud of your fuck ups. Your fuck ups are how you learn. Now I really sound like a life coach. Oops.

Through my many missteps throughout the dance of life, I've learned several things I call universal truths. Although the funny thing about the truth is that it's subjective. Have you ever argued with someone on Facebook? Then you know what I mean. The truth belongs to the one who believes it. If that makes sense. And if it doesn't, that's OK. I have some stuff I need to cover before this book ends.

In order to live the best possible life, you should probably subscribe to the OWN channel on cable. I understand that Oprah has guests and shows and programming that is meant to uplift you and inspire you. I don't think I am capable of doing either.

But then again, I never said I wanted to be a life coach. If you skipped that page earlier, the only really useful advice I could give you is: Don't Be an Asshole.   Many times in my own life I have been a complete and utter asshole. I'm not referring to accidental assholeness. I'm talking about those times I did it on purpose.

Besides that, do you know what life coaches charge? I think it's more than a therapist, and they don't even have to have any legitimate training. Sure, every life coach I've ever met rattled off a bunch of affiliations that I never understood, and to be honest, sounded made up. If you find yourself wanting a life coach, you should just grab a friend, share some booze, and watch how quickly the truth starts coming out. Much cheaper! More fun!

As a non-life coach, I'll admit I don't believe in regrets. There have been numerous events in my life I would never wish to remember, but I'm not sorry those things happened. It would totally nullify my twenties! Besides, it gives me so much material to draw from.

Sometimes life was kind and because of the magical sorcery of alcohol, they've been totally wiped from my memory all together. Being old as hell, I have joyfully lived most of my years on this earth free of the threat of being secretly filmed and put on YouTube.

Imagine a world in which you could act like an idiot, and not become an embarrassing internet sensation? Oh, what a truly remarkable time to be alive.

Because of all the cool stuff I've done and screwed up, you might imagine I have a lot more things to tell you before we part ways. They are random and stupid, and speak for themselves, so rather than having a bunch of separate chapters, I figured I'd roll all my mistakes into one epic ending. You're welcome.

DON'T BELIEVE THE GPS (lying electronic demon)

There are a lot of things you shouldn't believe. Take GPS for example. When I travel to Seattle, a beautiful city, I use the Space Needle to help me navigate. That only works when you're downtown or downtown adjacent. When the needle is out of sight, GPS would seem like a safe alternative. But GPS can lie.

My daughter and I were going round and round in a circle of one-way streets, trying to get somewhere specific, though I couldn't tell you where. Like the dreamers we were, we plugged in our location and destination. My daughter barked out the directions that the evil GPS gave her, and round and round we went. I finally pulled off into an empty parking lot, after the third go round.

"Find out where we are!"

"Mom, it can't be right. It says we are 'nowhere' and we are definitely somewhere."

She wasn't exaggerating. GPS decided we were nowhere. Where do you go from nowhere? Throw the GPS out the window. That's a start.

SLEEPING WITH CO-WORKERS

Maybe it's obvious. I don't think you should sleep with your co-workers. It never ends well and sometimes creates a hostile work environment. At the very least, when you leave or get fired, your snarky, vengeful co-workers will spread it around. I can say this from experience, and I really wish that my personal emails hadn't been forwarded around the office – but hey, I don't work there anymore! Assholes.

Maybe the obvious thing to add is: don't use work email to send personal stuff that can be held against you. Oops.

BE NICE TO THE KIDS

Did I need to say it? Maybe to make myself feel like a better person. Obviously, I don't think it's ever OK to say mean things about kids. Your own kids, or other people's kids. Either way it's just wrong. Children are our future, and you should cut them some slack. If you want to talk smack about their parents, who are probably screwing them up, that's totally legit.

There are people who over post pictures of their kids, grandkids, nephews. They fill up your newsfeed when what you're really on Facebook for is to get into political arguments with strangers, don't they know that? How dare they!

After years in the field of public relations, I have found a universal solution that applies to any situation involving someone else's kid. They did something you think is stupid? You simply respond, "Isn't Johnny spirited!" You think their school picture is laughable? Say, "Look at your little ray of sunshine!" Ugly baby? Easy peasy. "Look, it's a baby!"

It goes a long way, saying nice things, even when you might not mean them. I promise you, using a filter every once in a while, is not the worst thing you can do for friendships and family.

DON'T TEXT THE EX

Listen, your ex might be a perfectly lovely person. Probably not, or they wouldn't be your ex. But let's pretend they aren't a tool. Unless you're texting to get back your underwear (just kidding, let that shit go!), or you need to work out a visitation schedule regarding your dog (just kidding, don't share a pet!), you should maintain a safe distance.

Boundaries are a great thing. People tell me I have none, so I plan on getting some. From what I understand, boundaries keep things from getting messy. They make sure that we all stay in our own lane. Once someone is an ex, whatever they do, whomever they do, is really none of your business.

You can't move forward if your eyes are fixed on the rearview mirror. You're not going in that direction, my friend! Maintain your boundaries, keep your head in the present, and keep pushing forward. I'm not saying you and your ex can't be friends. I am friendly(ish) with at least a handful of mine. But if you don't maintain those boundaries, suddenly you're flirting again, getting close again, and you might end up naked together.

Just because something is familiar to you, doesn't mean it's good for you. That's what people tell me anyway. So maybe, don't text the ex. Go out with your friends instead, and fantasize about the next hot mess who is going to pull into your driveway.

DON'T TAKE ANY OF THIS TOO SERIOUSLY

I think by now, you and I have been on a short journey together. You've made it this far, and presumably not cursed my name and thrown this book against the wall. I use humor to rant, to deflect, and to tell a fabulous yarn.

Clearly, I don't take life very seriously. You probably shouldn't either. I mean sure, we are expected to go to work, and pay bills, maybe even raise our own children (gasp!). We develop coping strategies, like yoga, psychotherapy, or drinking...whatever hobby works. We all have to cope in our own ways because none of us can predict the twists, turns and horrible surprises around every corner.

If you want to feel happy...I have no idea what you should do. Happy is totally subjective and everyone decides for themselves what that is, am I right? If you're taking a page out of my book (punny!), you need to absolutely, unequivocally not care what anyone else thinks.

If you have a boss, or a horrible mother-in-law, maybe your life would be easier if you developed thick skin and said and did the things that make **them** happy. Since I have neither of those people in my life, I feel absolute freedom to act as inappropriately and freely as I like.

Sure, I've embarrassed the hell out of my children more times than I can count. Maybe it's not a coincidence that both of my daughters have changed their names! I admire their moxie, probably more than they admire mine.

The one piece of advice I feel totally qualified to give is:

DO WHAT YOU WANT

Listen, I am not a particularly wise person, not particularly successful, and certainly not all that wealthy if we're using my bank account as a measure. What I can tell you is that we all struggle with our own little bit of madness. Anyone who tells you they don't lose their shit from time to time, is either a liar, or a complete sociopath and you don't need that kind of negativity in your life.

It's OK to sit back and reflect every now and then, and wonder how you survived as long as you have. I like to do that regularly, and it doesn't always involve a cocktail, but 98.2% of the time it definitely does. You've accomplished a great deal in your life. If you have lived past the age of 27, you basically deserve a medal.

We all know about the unfortunate 27 Club -- the age when so many rock stars and famous folks have checked out: Kurt Cobain, Jimi Hendrix, Janis Joplin, Amy Winehouse, Jim Morrison...ugh. Do you need a drink yet?

My point is, this life of yours might be really long or it could end next week. While you are here on this planet of smog and pollution, and green trees, and global warming, and humanity, and cruelty, and war, and peace, and hope, and politics, and the oxford comma, it's yours to live as you see fit. And if other people don't like it, they can pretty much piss off.

Sorry, that almost sounded self-helpy. I am anything but a helper. But still, do it your way. **Own this bitch.**

Buy the car you want. Take the job you want. Move into the house you want. Talk to the girl or guy that you want. Get the tattoo that you want (maybe don't get a name or initials!). Marry who you want. You're going to be dead eventually, maybe even soon.

Until that day, it's your life. Do whatever makes you happy, or something closely resembling that. I mean, don't be an asshole, of course. But beyond that, go wild!

Just don't blame me.

ABOUT THE AUTHOR

Rosalie Brown is no super hero, just another cynical passenger on
the life raft. She had lots of fun in her twenties, marginal fun in
her thirties, and is currently limping through her forties.
Naturally, she totally digs her daughters, her dog,
Pearl Jam concerts, and getting caught in the rain.
Any adventures mentioned in this book did in fact happen,
but she's not holding any grudges. However, she is taking notes.

www.dontblameme.xyz

www.ingramcontent.com/pod-product-compliance
Lightning Source LLC
Chambersburg PA
CBHW061152040426
42445CB00013B/1656